CAIRNPAPPLE HILL

Gordon Barclay and Doreen Grove

EDITED BY CHRIS TABRAHAM
ILLUSTRATED BY DAVID HOGG AND DAVID SIMON
PHOTOGRAPHY BY HISTORIC SCOTLAND PHOTOGRAPHIC UNIT
DESIGNED BY MAGNUS DESIGN
PRINTED IN SCOTLAND FROM SUSTAINABLE MATERIAL
BY BUCCLEUCH PRINTERS LTD., HAWICK

FIRST PUBLISHED BY HISTORIC SCOTLAND 1998
REPRINTED 2007
CROWN COPYRIGHT © HISTORIC SCOTLAND 1998
ISBN 1 900168 56 1

INTRODUCTION

"Cairnpapple stands virtually alone in British archaeology in offering evidence of such long-sustained religious observance at a particular spot; it thus has a virtually unique claim to being a holy place."

(Rodney Castleden, *Neolithic Britain* 1992)

Cairnpapple Hill is one of the best known prehistoric sites on the mainland of Scotland. It is perhaps unwise to go as far as Mr Castleden in assuming a religious use for Cairnpapple and implying a parallel with modern churches. But he is undoubtedly right in stressing that it was a spot known and revered by the people who lived in its shadow for thousands of years. The site consists of both ceremonial and burial monuments.

People first left left traces of their activity on Cairnpapple Hill about 5500 years ago; they lit fires and left pottery and axes on the site. The same type of evidence has been found on comparable sites excavated in Scotland. These people were farmers in the valleys below the hill, and they lived in a time archaeologists today call the early Neolithic.

The second period of activity at Cairnpapple Hill was also the grandest. It probably began about 5000 years ago, in the later Neolithic, with the building of a henge monument. Construction on so large a scale must have been a communal effort and the henge probably had a ceremonial use.

Several centuries later, during the Bronze Age, the use of the site changed from ceremonial to burial. Whether the site became a cemetery because of its former sanctity, or despite it, we do not know. It is, however, a feature which Cairnpapple shares with many henge monuments, suggesting perhaps a new order 'hedging its bets' and relying on a little of the old 'magic' to help establish new traditions. Whatever the reason, there followed a lengthy period of burial at the site lasting over 2000 years. A variety of funereal practices was used. Burials were placed under cairns, in stone-lined boxes called cists, in shallow graves and in unlined pits. Some were cremations; others were interments of unburnt bones. A few were buried with belongings, mostly pottery vessels, but also including items of wood and animal bone. The latest burials on the site date probably from the post-Roman era.

These brief paragraphs carry us over the lives of 200 generations, farmers who worked the land below and beyond the Bathgate Hills and for whom Cairnpapple was a special place. It is perhaps no coincidence that the latest 'monument' on the hill is the modern radio mast, sited there because of the wide reception area it serves!

An aerial view of Cairnpapple Hill from the south-east.

CAIRNPAPPLE HILL IN CONTEXT

*T*he lives of our distant ancestors hold a powerful fascination for us. We know they had the same basic aims as we do; they needed to eat and sleep, and to provide their families with shelter and security. But each society has its own view of the world and of its place in it, views that we may find strange or even incomprehensible. Human life goes beyond the mundane of survival; all cultures structure their existence through ritual and ceremony. Our fascination with the Neolithic and Bronze Age is perhaps heightened because almost the only tangible features that survive from those societies relate to ceremonial or burial activities; we know very little of their everyday lives. On the principle that something as important to a community as Glasgow Cathedral or the Scott Monument is more likely to survive than a suburban house, it is perhaps not surprising that the grand public edifices of early prehistory survive better than the houses of the people who built them.

The henge monument at Balfarg, Fife, from the air. (Courtesy of Fife Council.)

At Cairnpapple Hill, this dilemma is obvious. We have the remains of a ceremonial site which was in use for a considerable time, yet no houses belonging to the Neolithic builders have been found in the immediate vicinity. To be able to make sense of the monument, we therefore need to use both the archaeological evidence found at Cairnpapple and that found at comparable sites, both near and far. The best parallels are provided by the henge complexes at North Mains, in Perthshire, Balfarg, in Fife, and others in northern England. In addition, we must glean what we can of the builders from the few Neolithic houses so far discovered - the village at Skara Brae in Orkney, and the remains of another Neolithic settlement a little nearer at hand, at Cowie, in Stirlingshire. However, we need to be careful about using information from one part of the country to interpret what is going on in another, because each area clearly had its own local traditions in building styles and pottery manufacture.

The subsequent use of the site for burial purposes is rather better served for parallels, and we know a little more of the lives of the people who lived in the shadow of Cairnpapple Hill in later prehistory.

A typical house in the Neolithic village at Skara Brae, Orkney.

EXCAVATION

Prior to the excavations by Professor Stuart Piggott in 1947-8, Cairnpapple Hill had received little attention. All that was visible was a grassy mound, sitting off-centre from a lightly-defined, almost circular, earthwork. Piggott's excavations demonstrated that the earthwork was a henge, a class of monument represented across the British Isles, from the Ring of Brogar and the Stones of Stenness, in Orkney, to sites in the south-west of England.

Cairnpapple Hill shortly before excavations began in 1947. (Courtesy of the Royal Commission on the Ancient and Historical Monuments of Scotland.)

When Piggott began his investigations at Cairnpapple, no henges had been scientifically excavated in Scotland. This left him with no option but to look south for clues and parallels to help him in his analysis. The site that, at that time, seemed to provide the best parallel to Cairnpapple was at Arbor Low, in Derbyshire. It occupied a similarly elevated position, an unusual feature as most henges are situated on low-lying land, and was of strikingly similar size and shape. The ring at Arbor Low, however, was formed of stone uprights whereas at Cairnpapple timber posts were used.

Since Piggott's time, a further six henges have been excavated, either wholly or in part, in Scotland. The results of this work have added immeasurably to our knowledge of the early prehistory in this part of Britain. But most importantly, the results allow us to take a fresh look at the evidence so ably collected by Professor Piggott, and to offer a re-interpretation of the site.

The henge at Arbor Low, Derbyshire, from the air. (Courtesy of English Heritage.)

Because so few of the features discovered during Piggott's excavation had any direct association with one another (a point Piggott himself was at pains to point out), there are many questions about the relationships between the features on the site which cannot be answered precisely. Unfortunately, radio-carbon dating had not been developed by 1947; if it had been, the charcoal from the site could have been dated with reasonable precision. The more recently-excavated sites, by contrast, have benefited from such dating techniques.

Piggott's phasing of the site relied heavily on ideas then commonly accepted, ideas which recent research has shown to be inaccurate. As a result, the original division of the site's occupation into five neat phases has now been replaced by a more simple, but less precise interpretation, based on the two uses of the site, first for pure ceremony or ritual, and thereafter as a burial place. The pre-henge use of the site is also consistent with evidence found at most of the henges excavated in recent years.

Excavating at Cairnpapple Hill 1947-8. (Courtesy of the Royal Commission on the Ancient and Historical Monuments of Scotland.)

THE HENGE BUILDERS

Who were the people who built the henge some 5000 years ago; what were they like and where did they live? The evidence, alas, is sparse. We know that they were farmers who lived and toiled in the valleys around Cairnpapple Hill. Farming folk had been in the locality for hundreds of years prior to the henge being constructed. They cleared part of the land of trees and scrub, and then cultivated with spade and hoe, possibly even the plough. Each year they planted cereal crops, and each year they harvested. They kept cattle, pigs, sheep and goats, and they supplemented their diet by hunting and fishing. The boundaries of their fields, or plots, may have been marked out in some way, and the plots immediately around their homes were probably farmed more intensively than the outer fields.

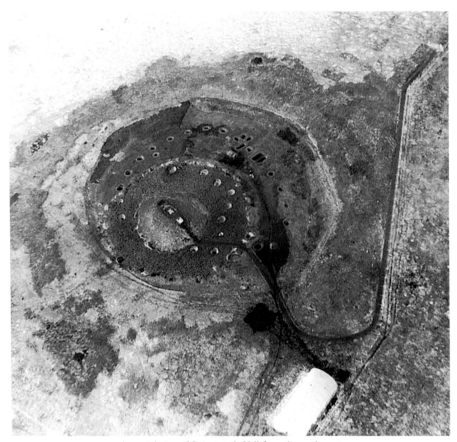

An aerial view of Cairnpapple Hill from the south-west.

What these homes looked like remains a mystery, for Neolithic houses have proved very hard to find. The little that we do know suggests that people in the later Neolithic, around the time of the building of the henge, were living in more rounded houses than those in the early Neolithic. They were constructed of the most plentiful material to hand. The Orcadians, for example, built their houses of stone, which is why they have preserved far better down the millennia. Elsewhere, low rubble walls and timber were used. In the area around Cairnpapple Hill, the houses were probably built entirely of timber, with a timber and turf roof.

The settlement probably consisted of more than one family but were not so big that we can think in terms of a village. They were invariably sited near a good water source, either a burn, loch or spring. Between the houses was a yard, with storage areas for fuel and fodder. There was probably also an area set aside for small-scale industrial activity; elsewhere, archaeological excavations have found evidence for flint knapping, the skinning and butchering of animals, leather working and basket weaving.

Major building projects like Cairnpapple clearly represent a significant investment in time and effort. Therefore, there must have been sufficient surplus food and other resources to allow investment on such a scale. It is also worth remembering that the people around Cairnpapple Hill did not live in splendid isolation but were part of a wider community, and at least some of their belongings came from far away, most obviously the stone axes which were brought from distant Wales and Cumbria.

Fragments of Neolithic axes of Graig Lwyd stone from North Wales (left) and Langdale Pike stone from Cumbria. (Courtesy of the Trustees of the National Museums of Scotland.)

BEAKERS AND BURIALS

Some considerable time after the construction of the henge, there appear to have been significant changes in the nature of the society using Cairnpapple Hill. This resulted in the site taking on a different meaning - as a burial site rather than as a place purely for ceremony or ritual. The first burial was placed in an extravagantly monumental grave (the north grave), suggesting that it may have been constructed for a very important person. The individual, whoever he or she might have been, was buried with great pomp and ceremony. The body was strewn with flowers and accompanied by prestige grave-goods, including a wooden club and Beaker pottery, a very distinctive decorative pottery.

So why did the use of the site change, and what if anything can this tell us about the community? The early burials were certainly placed within the henge, so the community was well aware of its importance. Perhaps we are observing a change of traditions in an existing community, and not the arrival of incomers. The objects buried

The Bronze-Age north grave after excavation in 1947-8.
(Courtesy of the Royal Commission on the Ancient and Historical Monuments of Scotland.)

along with the bodies point to strong trade links, goods and ideas as well as new technology. The earliest metal objects were imported from Europe, as perhaps was the skill to manufacture them; and Beaker pottery was also introduced, though it was very quickly given a local style. Throughout the later Neolithic and early Bronze Age, we see a greater emphasis on displaying the status of the individual in death than in the earlier period, culminating in some places in the erection of a monumental round barrow covering a single person. Such high-status burials have been found at North Mains, Perthshire, and at Clava, near Inverness.

One of the two Beakers discovered in the north grave during excavation in 1947-8.

Alongside these practical movements, one impetus for change, or the effect of it, may have been a new ideology or religion. It is so often the most compelling cause of cultural change.

We know little more about the lives of the early Bronze-Age inhabitants of the Cairnpapple area than we do of their Neolithic predecessors. Only one thing is known for certain: they remained farmers. However, the introduction of metals is not the only technological advance to emerge from the archaeological record. The first cartwheel in Britain, dated to the late Bronze Age, came from the Forth valley, to the north of the Bathgate Hills. Similar advances can be seen in agriculture; an ox-yoke found in Argyllshire is the oldest evidence in Britain for traction animals, almost certainly used for ploughing as well as pulling cumbersome carts.

There were many burials at Cairnpapple Hill throughout the Bronze Age. Some were quite simple – almost unmarked graves – whilst others were incorporated into monumental mounds clearly intended to be seen from a distance. Of the three successive cairns on the site, the north grave has no real parallels, but the two cairns built over it, which had mounds of stone or soil edged by a kerb of loose stones, follow patterns seen elsewhere in Scotland.

The remains of one of the three wooden disc wheels found at Blairdrummond Moss in the Forth valley in the nineteenth century and subsequently radio-carbon dated to the end of the second millenium BC. (Courtesy of the Trustees of the National Museums of Scotland.)

A SHORT TOUR OI

Note: Following the excavations in 1947-8, Cairnpapple Hill was laid out for visitors. The challenge of protecting the north grave (see 4) and the cist burials (see under 5) was met in 1949 by building a concrete dome on the footprint of the second cairn (see 5). This served both to protect the burials, and to allow public access to them. However, visitors should remember that the north grave was not contemporary with the cist burials and was

1. HENGE BANK AND DITCH

A NEOLITHIC MONUMENT, WITH AN OUTER, OVAL-SHAPED BANK ENCIRCLING A DITCH. THE EARTH FROM THE DITCH WILL HAVE FORMED THE BANK. THE BANK AND DITCH HAD TWO ENTRANCES ORIGINALLY, ALMOST OPPOSITE EACH OTHER. THE DITCH WAS PARTLY FILLED IN WHEN THE LAST BURIAL CAIRN [SEE 6] WAS BUILT.

2. HENGE POST HOLES

THESE ORIGINALLY HELD MASSIVE UPRIGHT POSTS, PROBABLY OF TIMBER. THE HOLES WERE PARTLY COVERED BY THE LAST BURIAL CAIRN [SEE 6]. FOLLOWING THE EXCAVATIONS OF 1947-8, THE HOLES WERE LEFT EXPOSED AND DEFINED BY RED GRAVEL.

3. ALIGNMENT OF HOLES

THIS ALIGNMENT OF THREE LINES OF HOLES MAY HAVE HELD UPRIGHT POSTS, POSSIBLY FOR A SCREEN. SEVERAL OF THE HOLES HAD CREMATIONS INSERTED INTO THEM, OR PLACED VERY CLOSE TO THEM. THE ALIGNMENT SEEMS LIKELY TO BE LINKED TO THE BUILDING OF THE NORTH GRAVE [SEE 4].

4. NORTH GRAVE

THE FIRST BURIAL AT THE SITE, OF BRONZE-AGE DATE. ORIGINALLY COVERED BY A SMALL CAIRN OF STONES BUT NOW DISPLAYED IN THE NORTHERN PART OF THE MODERN CONCRETE DOME ALONG WITH THE LATER CIST BURIALS [SEE UNDER 5]. THE

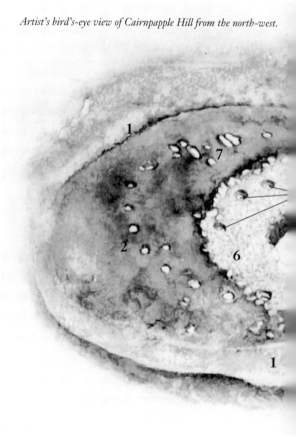

Artist's bird's-eye view of Cairnpapple Hill from the north-west.

CAIRNPAPPLE HILL

originally covered by a much smaller stone cairn. Around the dome, the remainder of the site was laid out rather like an exploded diagram, with coloured gravels used to identify the different periods of construction. Of course, none of the users of Cairnpapple would ever have seen it thus, but this presentation of the site does allow its complicated history to be viewed all at once.

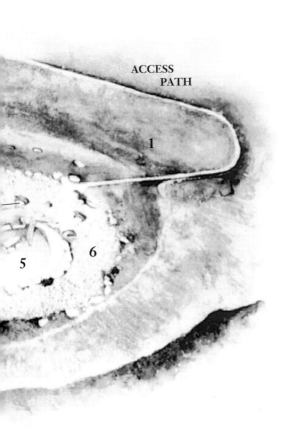

GRAVE, DEFINED BY AN UPRIGHT STONE AND AN OVAL STONE KERB, CONTAINED EVIDENCE FOR A FULL-LENGTH BODY, THE REMAINS OF A WOODEN OBJECT, POSSIBLY A CLUB, AND TWO BEAKERS.

5. SECOND BURIAL CAIRN
CONSTRUCTED AFTER THE NORTH GRAVE [SEE 4]. NOW DEFINED BY ITS LARGE KERBSTONES AND BY THE MODERN CONCRETE DOME ERECTED OVER IT AFTER 1948. INTERRED IN THE CAIRN WERE TWO CIST BURIALS, THE LARGER ONE WAS THE FOCUS OF THIS CAIRN AND HAS A CUP-MARKED STONE. [THE CONCRETE DOME IS MUCH HIGHER THAN THE ORIGINAL CAIRN WOULD HAVE BEEN.]

6. LAST BURIAL CAIRN
THE LAST BURIAL CAIRN TO BE BUILT, THIS WAS DOUBLE THE SIZE OF ITS PREDECESSOR [SEE 5]. IT IS NOW DEFINED BY ITS OUTER KERB AND A LARGE SPREAD OF STONE RUBBLE. A CENTRAL BURIAL FOR THIS CAIRN WAS NOT FOUND, BUT TWO CREMATIONS, BOTH CONTAINING CINERARY URNS, WERE DISCOVERED SET INTO THE SIDES OF THE CAIRN.

7. LATE BURIALS
FOUR GRAVES, ALIGNED EAST-WEST, AND SO PROBABLY EARLY CHRISTIAN IN DATE, OCCUPY THE EASTERN HALF OF THE HENGE. THEY ARE NOW FILLED WITH LIGHT GRAVEL.

THE ARCHAEOLOGY OF CAIRNPAPPLE HILL

THE EARLIEST EVIDENCE

The first traces of activity at Cairnpapple date from some 5500 years ago. However, nothing of this period is now visible at the site. Indeed, even within the archaeological record the traces are very slight. Six hearths were discovered during the 1947-8 excavations; one was under the bank of the henge, so it at least must pre-date the building of the henge. The others were similar, but they need not necessarily be of the same date.

The hearths were used for small fires of oak and hazel. No artefacts were found in them, but two pieces of Neolithic pottery (both from round-bottomed bowls, one plain and the other lugged) and two fragments from stone axes were found on the old ground surface within the henge. One of the axes had come from the axe-factory at Graig Lwyd, in Wales, and the other from Great Langdale, in Cumbria.

The hearths and their accompanying finds, all dating to between 5500 and 5000 years ago, represent the sum of early Neolithic activity. This may seem a thin collection of evidence to base a phase of activity upon; however, traces of this sort of pre-henge activity are now too common to dismiss out of hand. They have been found on virtually every other henge site excavated in Scotland in recent years. At Balfarg, in Fife, (see the photograph on page 4) for example, the pre-henge use of the site included pits lined with broken pots and sealed with layers of boulders.

Artist's impression of early Neolithic people lighting fires and burying potsherds at the site, based on the evidence from Balfarg.

THE HENGE MONUMENT

The ceremonial use of the site moved from the ephemeral to the more tangible about 5000 years ago with the construction of the henge monument. The elements that made up the henge monument were a bank and ditch, and a ring of 24 upright timber posts in the interior. The bank and ditch must surely be contemporary with each other, but that need not necessarily have been the case with the uprights; these may have been erected before, during, or conceivably soon after the henge itself. There would appear to have been some focus of activity in the western half of the interior of the henge.

The henge bank measures 60 m from crest to crest. Excavation showed that at its base was a layer of clay laid directly on the old ground surface. Turf from the top of the ditch was then laid on the clay, and the remainder of the bank was built up of the excavated soil and stones from ditch. The ditch was over 1 m deep, except on the east side where it was slightly shallower because it had been cut through the basalt rock. The bank on excavation stood to 1.2 m in places, but originally it was probably a little taller than an adult; it has been suggested that one of its main functions was to mask the interior from prying eyes! It was not a uniform width, being in places almost 6 m thick. The level berm between the ditch and bank was about 4 m wide, and the ditch was about 4 m across the top.

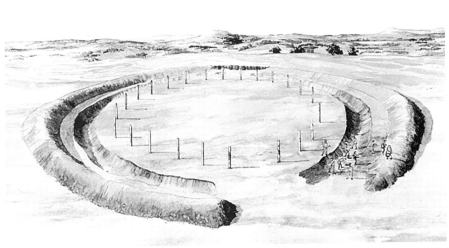

Artist's impression of the henge monument being created.

Ditches could have been dug in two ways; either a number of gangs worked simultaneously on different parts of the ditch, or one gang started at one end, by digging a hole, and then working to a face. Each method would leave different traces, detectable through archaeological excavation. The henge ditch at Cairnpapple seemed to be made up of joined pits, which would indicate that the former method was more likely to have been used.

The henge had two entrances, almost opposite each other in the north-east and south-east quadrants, and both measuring about 9 m across. The excavations did not extend far enough to examine whether the entrances had evidence for timber screens across the entrances, such as have been detected at another henge and which were thought to have helped screen views of the interior. (Because the banks and ditches were not totally excavated in 1947-8, it is not now easy to trace these entrances on the ground; however, the present path to the cairn passes through the southern entrance.)

The circle of 24 upright posts lay immediately inside the bank and ditch, although the ring did not entirely follow the line of the ditch. This may simply be an indication that the relationship between the two was not considered important, or that the laying-out was inaccurate, or even that the circle pre-dated the ditch. When first excavated, the uprights were thought to have been of stone. However, evidence from elsewhere indicates that this was probably not the case. The size and shape of the holes lend themselves to having held massive timber uprights, perhaps a little taller than an adult. There is no evidence that they were connected to one another in any way, though that possibility has been suggested at other henges. The builders could have created a ring quite simply by using cross-pieces of wood or rope.

The large, oval interior of the henge must have been the sacred centre of whatever ceremonies were practised here. We know nothing of the nature of such ceremonies, or where within the interior they took place. It is possible that some focus of worship, within an arrangement of either stones or timbers, lay in the western half of the cairn, under where the concrete dome stands today. However, the evidence was very slight - just shallow pits and hollows and no way of knowing how they might have been used or whether they held uprights of stone or timber.

We do not know who was allowed to enter the henge, but there would have been little point in screening off the interior from view if just anyone could go in. It is conceivable that there were certain, special individuals who officiated at the ceremonies, and other privileged members of the community who were permitted to attend them.

The Ring of Brogar henge in Orkney with its impressive circle of upright stones, 60 in all. This henge is also in Historic Scotland's care.

DEATH AND BURIAL

About 4000 years ago, the henge ceased to be used for ceremonial purposes. However, it remained in use. The local community must have revered it sufficiently for they buried an important member of their community there. It may be coincidence, but the spot they chose, in the western half, was where evidence had been found for an earlier ceremonial use. This first burial cairn is known as the north grave.

The **north grave** is impressive by any standards. It was the final resting-place for a single individual. The grave is rock-cut and lies within an oval setting of stones, measuring 3.3 m by 2.7 m; beyond it may have been a larger kerb. The west end of the grave is marked by a massive upright stone nearly 2.4 m high, and over the grave was piled a low stone cairn, perhaps gathered from some of the shallow, featureless pits discovered within the henge.

Because of the acidity of the soil, the only remnants of the body to survive were slight stains on the floor of the grave and the enamel crowns of the teeth. These showed that the corpse had been laid out at full length. It had probably been wrapped in organic material, perhaps grass-matting of some sort. The face had been covered by a carefully

The upright stone, kerbs and burial pit of the north grave in the western part of the henge. This first burial at the site, originally covered by a small stone cairn, was later incorporated within a larger cairn.

placed burnt wooden mask and alongside the body was another piece of burnt wood, about 1 m long, possibly a club. The grave may have been liberally strewn with seasonal flowers. Two Beaker pots, one with a wooden lid, had been left full of food or drink, perhaps to sustain the occupant of the grave on his or her journey to the next life. Evidence from elsewhere has shown that grave vessels occasionally held a cereal-based drink, possibly alcoholic, or porridge.

There was a **second grave** within the henge also containing a Beaker. This grave was smaller, indicating that it may have been intended for a child rather than an adult. Fragments of Beaker pottery were also found in the silt of the ditch. At the time that the north grave was built, it seems likely that the area to its east was in use as a cremation cemetery. This may have been bounded by the **three lines of pits** around the north-east, east and south-east sides of the north grave. These pits may have held timber posts, perhaps forming a screen.

Artist's impression of the north grave at the time of the interment.

Some time after the building of the north grave, a **cist burial** was placed next to it. This comprised several upright slabs forming a rock-cut pit, with a single massive capstone on top. Later disturbances had caused the capstone to be wrenched aside, and the west wall to tumble in, half filling the interior. A Food Vessel was found intact on the top of that fill. It had been carefully placed on a shelf at the top of the cist and only had a few centimetres to fall during the collapse. Close to this first cist burial was a **second cist burial**, also with a very large capstone but this one only 200 mm deep. The cist contained a single, unaccompanied human cremation. These two graves had been built about the same time, and they had then been covered by a **stone cairn**, 15 m across and neatly edged with 21 kerb stones. Two of the holes for the uprights of the henge were buried beneath this second cairn, showing that it post-dated the henge.

In the stones filling the central cist was one squarish block, almost certainly part of the collapsed west wall. It had three **cup-marks** pecked into its surface. This is a feature that can be seen on many early Bronze-Age cairns. Other cup-marked stones were found scattered in the make-up of the stone cairn. This cairn was replaced by a concrete dome in 1949, built both to protect the graves inside and to allow public access. The arrangement, well-intentioned at the time, is perhaps misleading, as it encourages the belief that the two cist burials were contemporary with the north grave, when they were in fact later and covered by a quite separate stone cairn.

The cist burial in the centre of the second stone cairn (foreground), with the earlier north grave beyond.

The Food Vessel in the central cist burial, as found during excavation. (Courtesy of the Royal Commission on the Ancient and Historical Monuments of Scotland.)

The Food Vessel from the central cist burial.

The **last burial cairn** to be built at the site was also the largest, with a diameter of about 30 m. It completely covered the two earlier cairns, but despite doubling the area of the cairn, it probably did not increase the height substantially. The construction of this last cairn consisted of smaller stones and a greater proportion of rubble and soil than the previous ones. On its west side, it overlay the by now silted-up ditch of the henge for a distance of 24 m. The cairn's kerb was also less well constructed; the boulders were smaller and rounder than the earlier kerb and were irregularly placed on the old ground surface. Seven of the post-holes from the henge uprights were also covered by the enlarged cairn, as well as some of the pits which may have been used for quarrying material for the previous cairns.

It is not at all clear what prompted the construction of this massive cairn. Primary burials were usually placed at the centre of cairns, but no such burial was discovered associated with this one. It is possible that this cairn was related to a burial, since destroyed, placed on the summit of the earlier cairn. **Two cremation burials** in upturned, collared cinerary urns, were found placed in pits cut into the cairn. At the burial on the west side, the urn had collapsed and the only grave-good retrieved was a burnt pin of deer antler. The second urn burial, on the south of the mound, also contained a burnt pin, this one an eyed, bone pin. Around the urn was a quantity of dark soil containing fragments of charcoal and burnt flint, suggesting that the remnants of the funeral pyre had been scooped up and deposited around the urn.

This latest, and largest, cairn is laid out around the base of the concrete dome. Within the make-up of the cairn, the upright post-holes of the earlier henge have been left visible and are filled with blue gravel.

Artist's impression of the third, and last, cairn being built. Its predecessor, the second cairn, is about to be buried under the rising piles of stone and earth.

Artist's impression of one of the cinerary urns being placed in the last cairn.

The cinerary urn found, upturned, over a cremation burial in the southern part of the last cairn.

Cairnpapple Hill from the north-west. The remains of the last cairn, with its massive stone kerbs, completely surrounds the grass-covered modern concrete dome which marks the position of the second cairn.

The **four graves in the eastern half of the henge** were the last in the burial sequence at the site. They are all shallow, rock-cut graves, lying roughly east-west. One of them had destroyed the greater part of one of the upright post-holes. The graves were long enough for fully-extended bodies, but no traces of bone or grave-goods were found. It is probable that the graves are of Christian origin, dating to the first millennium AD. Their occupants may well have been the descendants of the Neolithic farmers who first lit fires and deposited their axes here more than 3000 years before. This 'Christianising' of henge monments, and other ceremonial sites such as stone circles, is not uncommon. The graves are now marked in light gravel.

Artist's impression of one of the last burials, probably of Christian date, taking place at Cairnpapple Hill.

FURTHER READING

S Piggott, 'The Excavations at Cairnpapple Hill, West Lothian', *Proceedings of the Society of Antiquaries of Scotland*, 83 (1947-8) 68-123

P J Ashmore *Neolithic and Bronze Age Scotland* (1996)

K J Edwards & I B M Ralston *Scotland: Environment & Archaeology, 8000 BC - AD 1000* (1997)

G J Barclay *Farmers, Temples and Tombs* (1998)